THE COTSWOLDS

Stephen Dorey

CONTENTS

MYRIAD
LONDON

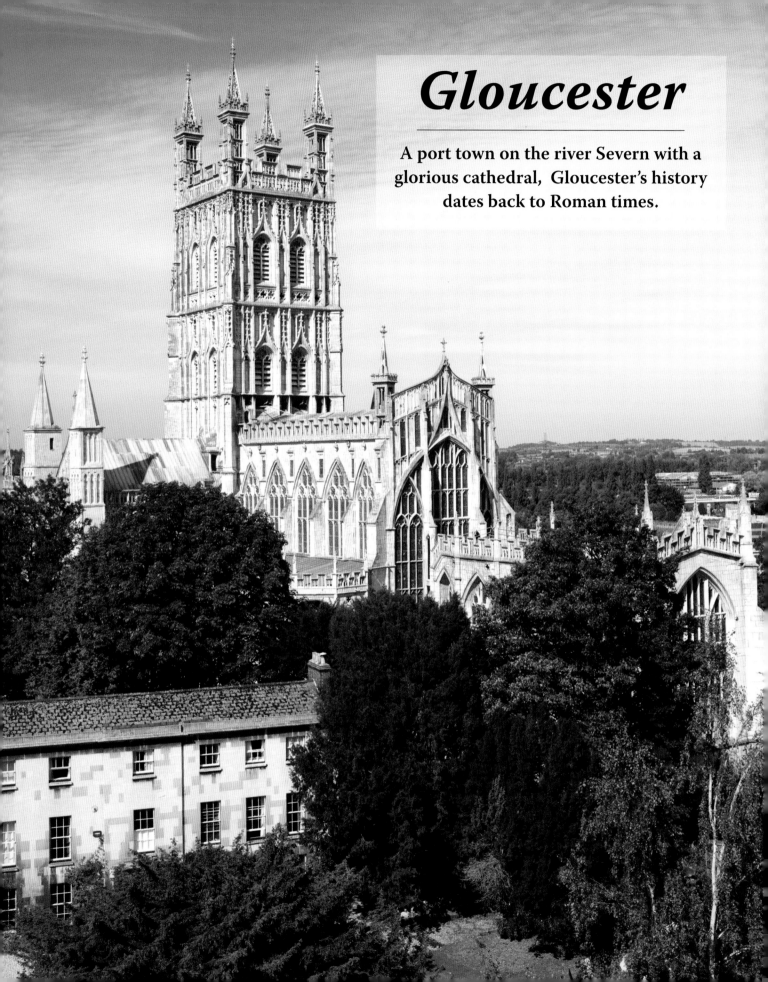

Gloucester

A port town on the river Severn with a glorious cathedral, Gloucester's history dates back to Roman times.

Built mainly on the eastern bank of the Severn and dating back to Roman times, Gloucester is sheltered by the Cotswolds to the east and the Forest of Dean to the west; the Malvern Hills protect the city from the north-west. The cathedral has its origins in an abbey founded in 681 and is the burial place of King Edward II. In the Middle Ages it was a centre for pilgrimage. Gloucester's long and prosperous history as a trading centre, inland port and spa can be glimpsed in the many fine buildings and churches that adorn the city.

GLOUCESTER DOCKS Opened in 1827, the docks allowed direct access by seagoing ships to Gloucester via the Severn estuary and a ship canal. At the docks goods could be transferred to canal barges for transportation throughout the Midlands. The docks and warehouses were further expanded in 1848 to cope with increased corn imports following the repeal of the Corn Laws. By the 1980s most commercial traffic had died away and the docks now provide spacious accommodation and ample leisure facilities. The survival of the old warehouses makes the main basin a popular location for filming period drama; fans of *The Onedin Line* will find the Biddle's warehouse familiar.

Cheltenham

This elegant town still retains much of its Georgian grandeur – a legacy of the time when Cheltenham was a fashionable spa resort.

The western edge of the Cotswolds is dominated by a large escarpment – the Cotswold edge – and by the river Severn and its tributaries which flow out of the surrounding hills. Just below the Cotswold edge lie Cheltenham and Gloucester two settlements quite different in character. Over the years both have expanded so that they now lie just a few miles from each other. The Severn has carved out deep and wide valleys and the prosperous towns on the flood plain benefit from their shelter. The estuary also gives access to the sea and Gloucester has a long history as a sea port.

The elegant spa town of Cheltenham retains an air of Georgian grandeur, a legacy of the Regency period when it was a fashionable place to take the waters. The discovery of a spring in 1716, of the area's health-giving waters at Bay's Hill meadow, close to the Ladies' College, gave rise to a sudden burst of popularity and affluence and the spa at Cheltenham soon began to rival Bath in its splendour. Much of the architecture and layout of today's town dates from this period. The Spa reached the pinnacle of its success with the celebrated five-week visit of George III in 1788.

CHELTENHAM'S HISTORY

The early settlements in the Cheltenham area were noted for their peacefulness and quiet prosperity but the discovery of a spring, in what is now Cheltenham Ladies' College, in 1716 gave rise to a sudden burst of popularity and affluence. During the Regency period Cheltenham Spa rivalled Bath in its splendour as the rich and fashionable came to take the waters. The composer George Frederic Handel and Dr Samuel Johnson were among the town's notable visitors. In the 19th century the passing trade of the Spa was gradually replaced by permanent residents – often, it is said, retired colonial officers suffering from liver complaints! The Regency passion for horse-racing is maintained today at Cheltenham racecourse at Prestbury Park, home to the annual Cheltenham Festival and Cheltenham Gold Cup, the most prestigious meeting in the National Hunt racing calendar. The first Cheltenham Festival was held on the course

in 1902 and has continued ever since The town retains many of its fine Regency features such as spacious squares, crescents, promenades and beautifully laid out formal gardens. These are to be found on either side of the striking tree-lined Promenade which also contains many shops and buildings. The source of Cheltenham's wealth can be seen in its neo-classical Pittville Pump Room complete with an elegant circular bandstand. As well as racing, Cheltenham hosts several major festivals each year, including those devoted to music, science and literature. On a more modern note, the GCHQ building is home to the government sur-veillance programme and is also located in Cheltenham.

CLEEVE COMMON Cleeve Hill and Cleeve Common form a broad expanse (about 1000 acres) of gently sloping open countryside just to the north-east of Cheltenham. West Down is located here; at 1082ft (330m), it is the Cotswolds' highest point. Magnificent views over the Severn Vale and the Malvern Hills are easily accessible from the scarp slope that rises out of Cheltenham. The area is popular with walkers and riders and there is plenty of wildlife to observe in addition to the more traditional Cotswold cattle and sheep. The common was an important grazing area during the Middle Ages and an earthwork known as the Ring provides evidence of Roman livestock husbandry.

HAILES The area around Hailes gives little clue to its vibrant past. The tranquil wooded pasture land was once the site of a Cistercian abbey that came into possession of a relic of the Holy Blood of Christ during the 13th century. Authenticated by the pope, the relic drew vast numbers of pilgrims to the area and the abbey prospered. At the Dissolution of the Monasteries the abbey was handed over to the king's agents in 1539. Nearby is a 12th century church with interesting medieval wall paintings.

SUDELEY CASTLE This well-preserved building has had a rather chequered history. There was a castle on the site in Norman times but this was replaced by Sir Thomas Boteler during the Wars of the Roses. In the Tudor period the castle became the home of Catherine Parr, and in the Civil War it was Prince Rupert's headquarters. Sudeley then fell into disrepair until it was acquired by the Dent family in 1837. Extensive restorations were carried out under Lady Emma Dent. Catherine Parr had married Thomas Seymour after the death of Henry VIII but she later died in childbirth. A portrait of Catherine and a love letter written by her to Thomas Seymour are preserved at the castle; her marble tomb in the chapel was designed by Sir Gilbert Scott.

WINCHCOMBE The unspoilt town of Winchcombe is tucked away into the Cotswold edge and is sheltered on three sides by pleasantly wooded hills. Winchcombe was one of the seats of the Saxon kings of Mercia and was later a county town until it was absorbed by Gloucestershire. In the Middle Ages its abbey was a place of pilgrimage for followers of the martyred St Kenelm. The abbey has now completely disappeared. Most of the buildings that distinguish the town today are largely the legacy of the Cotswold wool trade. The town also benefited from its proximity to Sudeley Castle when the castle was the seat of great magnates and a host for royal visits.

ST PETER'S WINCHCOMBE

At the centre of Winchcombe is St Peter's, a justly celebrated example of a Cotswold "wool" church. The original Norman church was rebuilt in the Perpendicular style between 1460 and 1470. The west tower has three stages and is surmounted by battlements, pinnacles and gargoyles. A series of grotesque heads adorn many parts of the exterior and a gilded weathercock was added in 1874. Inside the church there is a rather sad wall-mounted memorial to Thomas Williams of Corndean, who died in 1636. It contains a single kneeling effigy of William in painted stone but the figure of his wife, who remarried after his death, was never added. Major restoration took place during the Victorian period but happily the late medieval atmosphere of the church has remained intact.

LECKHAMPTON Despite becoming a suburb of Cheltenham, Leckhampton has managed to maintain its own character and charm. The old village grew up around Leckhampton Court (now a Sue Ryder Hospice) and its associated church, and both buildings are still very much in evidence today. The church has an elegant tower and spire and preserves some interesting brasses and memorials. At the end of the 18th century Brandon Trye, a local landowner, developed quarries in the area and built a horse-drawn railway to transport stone into Cheltenham. One particularly hard pillar of rock was left untouched by the quarrymen and is now known as the Devil's Chimney. In the 20th century the owner of the quarries tried to fence them off and restrict access to the nearby common. This led to a riot in which eight men were arrested and sentenced to hard labour. Public access to the common was secured in 1929 when it was acquired by Cheltenham town council.

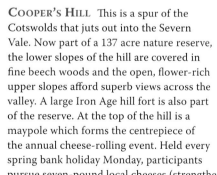

COOPER'S HILL This is a spur of the Cotswolds that juts out into the Severn Vale. Now part of a 137 acre nature reserve, the lower slopes of the hill are covered in fine beech woods and the open, flower-rich upper slopes afford superb views across the valley. A large Iron Age hill fort is also part of the reserve. At the top of the hill is a maypole which forms the centrepiece of the annual cheese-rolling event. Held every spring bank holiday Monday, participants pursue seven-pound local cheeses (strengthened with discs of wood) down a one-in-two slope. Winners are rewarded with the cheeses. Other activities on the day include uphill races. Many years ago the races were accompanied by morris dancing, wrestling matches and "girning" competitions. Girning required outstanding face-pulling abilities and, often, very few teeth. The eventual winners were presented with a horse collar.

BARROW WAKE This is
the site of the discovery of a
late Iron Age burial chamber
(*c*AD50) which revealed three
skeletons and a rich selection
of grave goods including the
justly famous Birdlip Mirror,
which can now be found dis-
played at the Gloucester City
Museum. Barrow Wake is
also a well-known viewpoint
on the Cotswold scarp that
offers panoramic views of the
Malvern Hills, the Severn Vale
and even glimpses of Wales.
The surrounding common
is a site of special scientific
interest in which unimproved
limestone grasslands support
over a hundred species of wild
flowers, including some rare
orchids. Twenty-two species
of butterfly have been identi-
fied on the site including the
comparatively rare Chalkhill
blue and the Duke of
Burgundy.

CRICKLEY HILL Fine views across the Severn Vale plus many areas of archaeological, geological and ecological interest make Crickley Hill a superb attraction. It is the site of a hill fort that was inhabited since Neolithic times. Extensive excavations in the area have revealed that the settlement was often refortified and may even have been the site of ancient conflicts. On the Iron Age part of the site is a defensive wall standing 12ft high but this has been reburied beneath the soil in order to preserve it. A visitors' centre provides information on all aspects of the area.

WITHINGTON The manor of Withington was formerly held by the bishops of Worcester and several of its buildings date back to the 15th century. The Mill Inn lives up to its name and has the river Coln running through its gardens, although no water wheel is present. At the centre of the village is a well-preserved Norman church. The exterior has many Norman features including a solid tower and splendid south doorway but unfortunately the interior was rather over-enthusiastically cleaned up during the Victorian period. A large Roman villa once stood in the area and a mosaic pavement from it is now in the British Museum.

CHARLTON ABBOTS The hamlet of Charlton Abbots is situated in the high country above the Isbourne valley and excellent views of the area can be gained from the village's churchyard. The church is Norman in origin but it was extensively restored in the 19th century. A short distance away there is a gabled manor house which dates from the Elizabethan and Jacobean periods. Both the rivers Isbourne and Coln have their sources in the area; the Isbourne flows north to join the Avon whilst the Coln flows south to join the Thames.

COLESBOURNE The wooded Churn valley, where the rather scattered village of Colesbourne can be found, is in contrast to the open country of Charlton Abbots. Colesbourne Park features numerous exotic trees as a result of the enthusiasm of a 19th-century squire, Henry Elwes. A keen botanist and forester, he scoured the world for specimen trees and planted many of them on his land at Colesbourne. Timber from the estate provided the bowsprit and masts of the restored SS *Great Britain*. Today the park is renowned for its carpets of snowdrops, now totalling 160 varieties, on display in February. The village church of St James is in the grounds of Colesbourne Park; it has a Perpendicular tower and in the interior there is a remarkable vase-shaped 15th century stone pulpit.

HAZLETON Like Turkdean and Notgrove, Hazleton's high position gives excellent views over the surrounding countryside. Its relative isolation means that Hazleton has changed little in recent years but the ancient Salt Way used to pass through it and it prospered during the medieval period as a result of the wool trade. The parish church is a Norman foundation but its tower and windows belong to the later Perpendicular period. The south doorway and chancel arch are Norman and there is a very solid 13th-century baptismal font. As in ancient times there is a great deal of foot and horse traffic around the village and excellent bridleways to Salperton in the north, Notgrove to the north-east and Turkdean to the east.

TURKDEAN Notgrove and Turkdean are in the high wolds and benefit from open fields and extensive views; however, they are also exposed to cold winds from the north. Turkdean is situated on a hillside with the hamlet of Lower Dean in the valley below.

LOWER HARFORD The Domesday Book mentions a village called Harford but it has long since disappeared, probably as a result of the extension of sheep grazing during the Middle Ages. The bridge and farmhouse at Lower Harford are pleasantly situated in the Windrush valley. The area is notable for its unusual breeds of domestic animals such as Cotswold Lion sheep and longhorn cattle. If they are not visible in fields these animals can be sighted in the nearby Cotswold Farm Park.

NAUNTON The straggling village of Naunton lies in the upper Windrush valley and can often be seen in its entirety from nearby hills. The village has been a centre for sheep-rearing since it became monastic land in the Middle Ages. This long history of animal husbandry means that this part of the Windrush valley is home to flowers found only on unimproved limestone pasture. In particular cowslips can be found in the spring, whilst yellow rattle and orchids adorn the fields in summer. Naunton's other industry was the production of stone roofing slates; at one time 30,000 a week were dug from thin stone seams in nearby mines. The industry declined from the middle of the 19th century when railways brought cheap slates from north Wales. The church has an imposing Perpendicular tower complete with pinnacles and gargoyles. Inside there is a carved 15th-century stone pulpit and a font from about the same period.

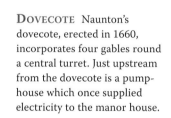

DOVECOTE Naunton's dovecote, erected in 1660, incorporates four gables round a central turret. Just upstream from the dovecote is a pump-house which once supplied electricity to the manor house.

GUITING POWER Lying near the confluence of the river Windrush and one of its tributaries, the name "Guiting Power" is derived from a mixture of the Old English *gyte*, which means an outpouring of water, and the name of the Le Poer family, the village's 13th-century owners. The majority of houses in Guiting Power are clustered around a sloping village green with the war memorial at its centre.

KINETON Between Temple Guiting and Guiting Power is the tiny village of Kineton. It combines attractive housing, including a traditional village pub, shady woodland walks and access to the upper course of the river Windrush. There are at least three fords in the area, two of which are close to the village. The lower ford is easily negotiated but the upper one requires some caution. The nearby Cotswold Farm Park is home to rare breeds of sheep, cattle, pigs and horses.

TEMPLE GUITING This attractive village is situated just upstream from Guiting Power on the western bank of the river Windrush. The Temple part of its name comes from the 12th century when the manor was owned by the Knights Templar. St Mary's church is built in an unusual combination of medieval and Georgian classical styles. Temple Guiting manor house was described by Pevsner as "one of the finest, if not the very best of the small Cotswold Tudor manor houses". Around Temple Guiting it should be possible to spot Cotswold Lion sheep in the fields. This large, white-faced, hornless breed was particularly prized in the Middle Ages for its long fleece and heavy wool. The wool produced was the foundation of most of the wealth in the area and the landscape of the Cotswolds owes much to this sheep husbandry.

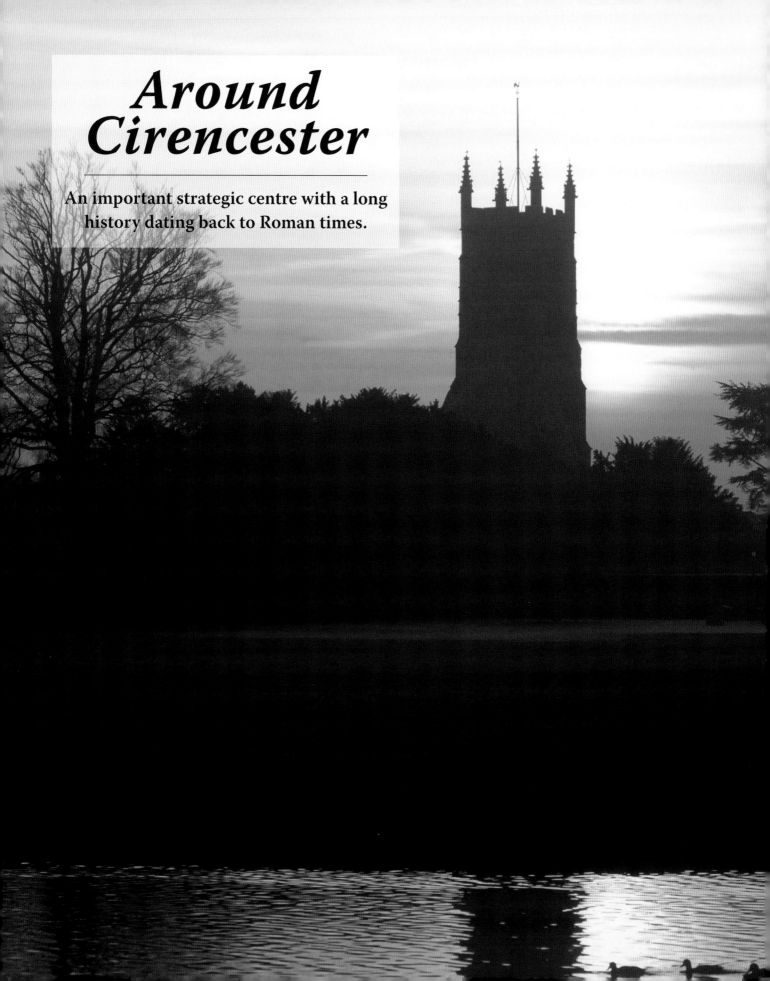

Around Cirencester

An important strategic centre with a long
history dating back to Roman times.

Cirencester was an
important city during
the Roman era and
stood at the junction of three
major roads: the Fosse Way,
the Ermin Way and Akeman
Street. The only visible
remains of the Roman city in
modern Cirencester are part
of the old town wall and an
impressive turf-covered
amphitheatre built in the early
2nd century. The town's prosperity in the Middle Ages was
aided by the presence of a
large abbey and it eventually
grew to pre-eminence in the
wool trade. Cirencester
remains a busy market town
and an important crossroads
in the southern Cotswolds.

CIRENCESTER At the centre of Cirencester is its marketplace which even today retains a great deal of the atmosphere of a busy prosperous Cotswold wool town. Rising above the marketplace is the 162ft (49m) high Perpendicular west tower of its parish church – the largest in Gloucestershire. The south porch, known as the Town Hall, has been used over the years as a tavern, schoolhouse and courtroom as well as the town's seat of governance. The church once belonged to Cirencester Abbey and after the Dissolution of the Monasteries it served as the town hall. The monks added the magnificent three-storey porch to the church at the end of the 15th century.

CIRENCESTER PARK

Occupying some 3000 acres, Cirencester Park is laid out geometrically according to Baroque ideas about landscaping. The scheme was begun by the first Earl Bathurst in 1714-18 and is still part of the Bathurst estate. The poet Alexander Pope advised the earl and his contribution is commemorated in a small rusticated shelter known as Pope's Seat. Other features added by the earl include the hexagon, a Doric column surmounted with a statue of Queen Anne and the Gothic folly of Alfred's Hall. The park is also famous as a polo ground.

BARNSLEY This elegant village is chiefly noted for Barnsley House Garden. Barnsley House itself dates from 1697 when it was built for a local landowner, Brereton Bouchier. It later became a parsonage but came to fame when Rosemary Verey took over its gardens in the 1950s. She created a variety of garden types including an 18th-century herb garden, a knot garden, a laburnum walk, a temple with pool and a vegetable garden.

THE AMPNEYS
This small group of villages is found, as their name suggests, on the Ampney Brook. Each has its own church and they must all have been thriving communities during the Middle Ages. The original parish of Ampney St Mary has disappeared making its church seem isolated. The present Ampney St Mary was formerly known as the hamlet of Ashbrook. The church of St Mary is a small Norman structure that still preserves many fascinating original features such as a carved lintel and medieval wall paintings. The church of the Holy Rood (an Anglo-Saxon word for cross) gives Ampney Crucis its name and there is a rare 15th-century cross in its grounds. To avoid its destruction, this was hidden from 17th century Puritans by being walled up inside the building.

AMPNEY ST PETER This is the third village in the group. Its church is mostly Saxon in design with some Victorian additions and there is a carved pre-Christian fertility symbol in the grounds. The largest house in the area is Ampney Park which was originally constructed for the Pleydell family in 1561; its extremely well-preserved Jacobean ceiling and oak-panelled walls are particularly noteworthy.

DOWN AMPNEY The birth-place of the composer Ralph Vaughan Williams, his father was the vicar of All Saints (below). Born in 1872 the young composer lived in what is now the old vicarage for the first three years of his life. He composed the hymn tune Down Ampney (better known as *Come Down Oh Love Divine*) in honour of the village.

BIBURY On the banks of the Coln, this ancient settlement dates back to Saxon times but most of the village owes its existence to the 17th-century wool trade. Arlington Row is a terrace of cottages that used to house workers from Arlington. Rack Isle, in front of the cottages and now a nature reserve, was originally used for drying wool. Alongside the traditional wool bale tombs in Bibury churchyard can be found Bisley Piece, a reminder of the 14th century when the people of Bisley angered a pope. Forbidden to bury their dead in their churchyard they had to travel 15 miles to use the tiny graveyard at Bibury.

WINSON The 49 houses that make up the village of Winson are situated to the west of the river Coln. There are many pleasant walks in the vicinity, either up the Coln valley to Coln Rogers or Coln St Dennis or down it to Ablington and Bibury. More adventurous walkers can head south over the wolds to Barnsley via Barnsley Park. In spite of its size the village possesses an imposing 18th-century manor house as well as a small church. The church is largely Norman but there are some 15th-century additions and Victorian improvements.

CHEDWORTH This interesting village combines sites of both ancient and modern interest. Opposite the ancient Seven Tuns Inn a spring emerges from a wall whilst elsewhere in the village there is a sculpture of the Virgin and Child carved by Helen Rock in 1911. The church retains some Norman features but it has been sensitively added to over the centuries. Not far from the village is Chedworth Roman villa. Discovered in 1864 and dating from AD120-400, the beautifully preserved remains include mosaic pavements (one depicting the four seasons), bath suites and a hypocaust. There is a small museum near the site.

YANWORTH Not far from the Chedworth Roman villa is the delightful village of Yanworth. Its Norman church stands slightly outside the village amongst a group of farm buildings. The church is chiefly remarkable for its 16th-century wall painting of a scythe-bearing Father Time. The village is on the Macmillan Way and makes a good starting point for walks to Chedworth to the south-west or Hampnett to the north-east.

NORTHLEACH This was one of the
most important Cotswold wool towns
in the Middle Ages and its heyday as
a medieval trading centre can still be
glimpsed in its market square and many
half-timbered buildings. The most
obvious legacy of Northleach's pre-
eminence in the wool trade is its
church. This was largely rebuilt in the
Perpendicular style in the 15th century
and is a magnificent example of the
style and period. The pinnacled south
porch is said to be without equal in
England and the tower combines both
elegance and strength. The generous
windows in the clerestory provide
ample light for such features as a 15th-
century goblet-shaped pulpit and a new
ceiling designed by Sir Basil Spence.
The church also has an extensive
collection of brasses which commemorate the wool merchants whose wealth
made the rebuilding and remodelling
of the church possible.

THE GREEN

CIVIC PRIDE Elsewhere in Northleach there are many other examples of civic pride and bene-faction. These include: a free grammar school founded in 1558; two sets of almshouses, one of which was exclusively for women; and a late 18th-century house of correction. This prison was built by local philanthropist Sir William Blackburn under the direction of the prison reformer Sir Onesiphorus Paul. It can be found at the crossing of the Fosse

Way just to the west of the main town. In the 18th century Northleach benefited greatly from being on a coaching route between London, Oxford, Gloucester and South Wales. It is said that Thomas Telford deliberately diverted the route through the town. Northleach did not have a sufficient water supply to take advantage of the Industrial Revolution and it went into serious decline during the early 19th century. In 1831 there were only 126 occupied houses and 795 inhabitants. It is hard to imagine such a dismal prospect in today's Northleach with its prosperous High Street and well-tended buildings. An unusual attraction is the World of Mechanical Music, a museum of music boxes, mechanical instruments and automatons.

CALMSDEN The hamlet of Calmsden is distinguished by a rare 14th-century wayside cross. Mounted on sturdy stepped stones the upright is still visible but the cross piece has disappeared. A spring emerges above ground nearby and a row of estate cottages built during the 19th century also add charm to the area. The Old House dates from the 16th century and is a classic example of Cotswold vernacular architecture. Calmsden is the starting point for many fine walks through both open and wooded countryside.

FARMINGTON The village of Farmington stands on high ground between the valleys of the river Leach and Sherborne Brook. The principal house in the village is Farmington Lodge. This is a mixture of 18th and 19th-century styles and is fronted by four sizeable Doric columns. A rather more graceful aspect of the village green is an octagonal pumphouse topped by an elegant cupola. This was restored and refurbished by the citizens of Farmington, Connecticut in 1931 to commemorate a long-standing connection between the two communities – a Farmington man is said to have fought at the Battle of Bunker Hill. The church is Norman in origin and still retains many Norman features such as its south doorway and chancel arch. The Perpendicular tower was added in the 15th century but is well integrated with the earlier buildings. A long barrow to the east of Farmington is at least 4000 years old while to the west Norbury Camp has provided both Iron and Stone Age remains.

NORTH CERNEY A pleasant village in the Churn valley north of Cirencester. The hospitable Bathurst Arms is *The Good Pub Guide* Inn of the Year 2011. The Norman church of All Saints has an unusual square saddleback roofed tower. The church has one of the finest interiors of any small Cotswolds church. In the Ladies Chapel are memorials to the Croome family, owners of Cerney House between 1810 and 1930. The house was built around 1660 and remodelled in a Georgian style in 1780. The lower floors were used as a hospital during the Second World War, whilst the owners, the De La Hay family, stayed upstairs. The garden has been restored to its former Victorian beauty by the present owners.

THE DUNTISBOURNES The four villages that bear the name Duntisbourne are strung out in a line along the Dun Brook. They are: Duntisbourne Abbots, Duntisbourne Leer, Middle Duntisbourne and Duntisbourne Rouse. Only Duntisbourne Abbots and Duntisbourne Rouse have churches. Today, Duntisbourne Leer is little more than a couple of farmhouses by a ford. The more interesting of the churches is the tiny church of St Michael in Duntisbourne Rouse. It has a Saxon nave and, because of the sloping ground, a small crypt chapel beneath the Norman chancel; this is unusual in such a small church.

BAUNTON This pretty village is situated on the river Churn. Its manor house dates from the 16th century and the original village school, which operated from 1849 until 1935, can still be seen at the Old School House. Other listed buildings in the village include Baunton Mill and Downs Farmhouse. The parish church, built originally as a chapel of ease by Augustinian monks, became the parish church in 1551 following the Dissolution of the Monasteries. Its shape and character have changed little over the years and the building preserves a large 14th-century wall painting of St Christopher ferrying the Christ Child across a river.

DAGLINGWORTH Sited along the Duntisbourne valley, Daglingworth is a popular starting point for short walks in the area. Some of the cottages have their own stone foot-bridges to allow passage across the brook. The church stands above the rest of the village to the south. Although it is Saxon in origin, it was extensively rebuilt in the 1840s. There remains a Saxon doorway and some striking Saxon carvings set into the walls. South of the village in the manor house grounds is a medieval dovecote which uses a revolving ladder to gain access to all of the 500 nesting holes.

North Cotswolds

Containing the market towns of Stow-on-the-Wold and Chipping Campden,
this area overlooks the Vale of Evesham to the north-west.

The Cotswolds are an undulating area of high ground with a steep scarp edge on the western edges. One of the largest towns in the area, Stow-on-the-Wold, boasts that it is the highest town in the Cotswolds, and most of the other neighbouring towns are on high ground. Locals will quickly tell you that this high altitude brings with it cold winds and unseasonable snow showers in early spring and late autumn. But for the visitor high vantage points and the many beautiful steep wooded valleys more than make up for this. The northern Cotswolds is classic sheep country and the fine market towns of Chipping Campden and Stow testify to the wealth which wool brought to this area.

SNOWSHILL There have been settlements near Snowshill since the Bronze Age. A barrow nearby contained a famous collection of weapons now in the British Museum. Snowshill was owned by Winchcombe Abbey from 821 until the Dissolution of the Monasteries. The main part of the current Snowshill manor house dates from around 1500. In 1919 the almost derelict building was bought and restored by Charles Paget Wade, who needed somewhere to present his collection of 22,000 examples of craftsmanship. The collection is extremely wide-ranging and includes automatons, butter stamps, bicycles, clocks, cowbells, locks and 26 suits of Samurai armour.

STOW-ON-THE-WOLD This distinctive settlement is the highest town, at 800ft (244m), in the Cotswolds. A popular rhyme begins, "Stow-on-the-Wold, where the wind blows cold", and the shape of its unusual market square is in part dictated by the need for stallholders to be protected from the wind. Despite its position, Stow-on-the-Wold has been a thriving market town since at least 1107 when it received its first royal charter. There were two annual fairs by the 15th century and Daniel Defoe reported the sale of 20,000 sheep in a single day there in the 18th century. In later years Stow-on-the-Wold became famous for its horse fairs, but nowadays the only

horses at the two charter fairs, one held in May and one in October, are likely to be on the merry-go-rounds. Stow-on-the Wold is also the site of one of the last major battles of the Civil War. A royalist march on Oxford with 3,000 men was thwarted by Cromwellian forces and 1,000 men were imprisoned in the church. Other disruptions to the town's peace are likely to have been dealt with in the town stocks.

UPPER SLAUGHTER Although it sounds bloodthirsty, the name Slaughter is probably derived from the Old English word *slohtre* meaning slough or boggy place. The two villages that bear the name are both beautifully situated on the upper reaches of the river Eye. They are only one mile away from each other, but they are very different in character. Upper Slaughter consists of cottages grouped around a small square with a church alongside; the cottages were reconstructed by Sir Edwin Lutyens in 1906. In spite of its name, Upper Slaughter is a double "thankful" village: all the men it sent to fight in the First and Second World Wars returned home alive.

LOWER SLAUGHTER The local manor house dates back to 1650 when it was built for Valentine Strong, the owner of a quarry at Little Barrington. The house has been remodelled since its construction but its grounds preserve one of the largest dovecotes in Gloucestershire. Several simply-built footbridges span the river Eye in Lower Slaughter. At one end of Lower Slaughter is a large millpond which feeds a working water wheel. The 19th-century mill – the Old Mill – is open to the public and houses a museum. The village hall was built in 1887 and provides a late Victorian attempt at a traditional Cotswold style. Also dating from the 19th century is St Mary's church which was rebuilt in 1867.

LONGBOROUGH This pleasantly situated village sits on a hillside overlooking the Evenlode valley. The church has a 13th-century tower with an added 15th-century upper section in the Perpendicular style. The church tower's six bells are referred to by Sir John Betjeman in his poetry collection *Summoned by Bells*. The windows of the south porch are in the Decorated style characteristic of the 14th century.

DONNINGTON Close to Stow-on-the-Wold is the hamlet of Donnington. It was here that the royalist Lord Astley surrendered after the Battle of Stow, one of the final actions of the Civil War. The hamlet gives its name to the nearby Donnington Brewery which supplies many Cotswold inns and pubs. The brewery has a working water-powered mill wheel.

LOWER AND UPPER ODDINGTON These twin villages form a single community on the slopes of a hill between Stow-on-the-Wold and the river Evenlode. Just south of the village is the church of St Nicholas. This dates from the 13th and 14th centuries and because of its relative isolation it largely escaped misguided attempts to improve it. The most striking feature of the interior is the extensive 14th century wall painting showing the Last Judgement and the torment of the damned. Created around 1340, the Doom painting occupies the entire north-west wall of the church. "Doom" paintings, designed to portray religious ideas to a largely illiterate population, were common features of medieval churches.

UPPER AND LOWER SWELL Upper and Lower Swell are associated with the river Dikler that rises nearby. At Upper Swell there is a small 18th-century bridge and beyond it a moss-covered weir which holds back an extensive millpond. The attached mill still has its water wheel. Further into the village there is a 16th-century manor house. Lower Swell has another bridge at its eastern end and features some fine 17th-century buildings. The church lies between the two villages. The original Norman building now forms its south side. Nearby are Abbotswood Gardens which were designed by the renowned architect Sir Edwin Lutyens. The gardens are often open to the public under the National Gardens Scheme.

MORETON-IN-MARSH Its strategic position straddling the Fosse Way and at the centre of various transportation routes made Moreton into a significant and prosperous town. During the 17th and 18th centuries it was on the main coaching route between London, Oxford, Worcester and Hereford. When coaching declined the town quickly moved on to railways; the Stratford-Moreton tramway opened in 1826 and was one of the earliest railways in the country. A mainline service arrived in 1843 and the line between London, Oxford and Worcester was opened in 1853. As a centre for travellers Moreton-in-Marsh is well provided with inns one of which, the 16th century White Hart (Royal) Hotel, was used by Charles I during the Civil War. It is also said to be haunted. The Curfew Tower on the corner of Oxford Street still has its original 1633 curfew bell hanging in it. The bell was in daily use until 1860 and even occasionally afterwards for summoning the fire brigade.

Three miles to the south-east is Chastleton House, a fine Jacobean manor house with much of its original furniture. Two miles from Moreton is the Four Shires Stone, a Cotswold stone pillar that marked the coming together of the four counties of Gloucestershire, Worcestershire, Oxfordshire and Warwickshire. County boundary changes have left the stone out of date.

MORETON-IN-MARSH MARKET Hand-in-hand with travel comes trade and Moreton has been an important market town for centuries. The first charter for a weekly market was granted to Moreton-in-Marsh in 1227 and in 1267 the town was granted a fair. A new charter was granted by Charles I in 1638. The ability to hold a market meant that the town benefited greatly from the influx of people but also that the town authorities could charge tolls and levies in return for services such as law enforcement.

The administrative centre for such activities was usually a market hall. The neo-Tudor style Redesdale market hall in Moreton-in-Marsh was built in 1887 and was designed by Sir Ernest George. More permanent trade was centred on the High Street with its stone-built shops, houses and coaching inns.

BOURTON-ON-THE-HILL Visitors to the Cotswolds might be forgiven for thinking that previous generations did not give a great deal of thought to place names. There are four Duntisbournes, three Ampneys and a profusion of places with Upper and Lower versions. Stow-on-the-Wold in Old English just means place on a hill. Bourton-on-the Hill is near Bourton Downs but confusingly it is about 10 miles from Bourton-on-the-Water. The village of Bourton-on-the-Hill was once owned by the abbots of Westminster who also had large sheep runs on the nearby downs. The wealth created by the 15th-century wool industry enabled the building of a fine clerestory on the local church of St Lawrence. The three-stage tower also dates from the Perpendicular period but the weighty arched columns of the interior reveal its Norman origins. The church also preserves a bell metal bushel, a 15th-century font and a peck from 1816. These standard measures were once required by law in every church so that they could be used for the gathering of tithes and for settling disputes. At the top of the hill is a substantial 18th century coaching inn. The village also contains many fine 17th and 18th-century cottages.

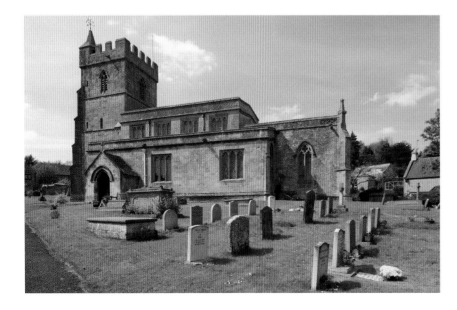

BLOCKLEY This was one of the first villages in England to produce its own electricity, thanks to the power of the Blockley Brook. In previous centuries the brook provided the energy for corn mills and silk throwers. Six mills once operated in the village although only one is still open; the beautiful Mill Dene garden has been created around another. Parts of the church date from the Norman period. Inside the church is a series of handsome monuments to local landowners and some interesting brass monuments to former priests.

BLOCKLEY SILK MILL At the height of the silk boom in the late 19th century there were six mills in Blockley and around 600 people were employed making silk for ribbon-making factories in Coventry. The old silk mill can still be seen beyond a pool near the church; the other mills are now converted into substantial private dwellings. Many of the terraced cottages on the northern edge of the village were once occupied by silk weavers.

CHIPPING CAMPDEN The word "chipping" relates to an Old English word meaning market and it was as a wool and cattle market that the village first grew up. The many fine houses in the town are evidence of its successful trading past. Grevel House was built for William Grevel in about 1380 and features striking Perpendicular-style two-storey windows. The market hall was built in 1627 and was intended for the sale of cheese, butter and poultry in a period when the wool trade was in decline. The row of almshouses just below St James' church dates from 1612; they originally cost £1,000 and are still used today to house 12 Campden pensioners. Next to the church are the lodges and gateway to Campden House. These are some of the only remains of the original buildings as the rest were burned down during the Civil War. St James' church is a local landmark. It is built in the Perpendicular style and features a 15th-century pinnacled tower.

BUILDING STYLES The growth and development of Chipping Campden over hundreds of years makes it a delight to the eye. In the gently curving High Street newer buildings were simply grafted on to older ones so that no two buildings are exactly the same and medieval buildings co-exist with houses in the Classical style. What gives the town its sense of unity is the use of golden Cotswold limestone whether in the sturdy arches of the market hall or in the lofty Perpendicular pinnacles of the church.

SILK MILL The old silk mill in Sheep Street is where CR Ashbee set up his Guild of Handicrafts in 1902. This involved moving 50 craftsmen and their families from the East End of London to Chipping Campden and setting them to work on traditional trades. Sadly this brave social experiment did not survive the rigours of the First World War and the Depression. Ashbee's workshop is now a small museum. One surviving remnant of the Guild is Harts Gold and Silversmiths.

WILLERSEY With its pretty green, duckpond and ancient church, Willersey is a picture-book English village. The village is on the edge of the Cotswolds but its mellow-stoned, well-proportioned houses link it firmly with many of the settlements of the high wolds. In the Middle Ages the abbots of Evesham had a summer residence in Willersey and later William Roper, the son-in-law of Sir Thomas More, owned the manor. King Charles II gave the Penderel family a house here in thanks for their help in his escape after the Battle of Worcester. Most of the houses in the village date from this period or later, although the church dates largely from the 14th century.

SAINTBURY This small village is ranged along the side of Saintbury Hill. The name Saintbury probably refers to a Saxon holy man called Cada who built a small cell nearby. The Norman church still preserves some fragments of a former Saxon building. The village itself features a fine cross which stands at the crossroads to the north of the village. The lower part dates from the 15th century whilst the Maltese cross and sundial were added in 1848.

BROADWAY Regarded by many as the finest large village in the Cotswolds, Broadway, as its name suggests, has a wide main street and the village was once an important staging post on the London to Worcester route. A new turnpike road was opened in 1736 and at one time seven coaches passed through the village every day. Many of the fine buildings along Broadway's main street began their lives as inns to serve the passing trade. With the coming of the railways the coach trade declined but Broadway had its own station and it quickly became a stopping off point for exploration of the Cotswolds.

Broadway Tower is built on the site of an ancient beacon and is said to have inspired JRR Tolkien to create the tower of Amon Hen and the Hill of Seeing in *The Lord of the Rings*. The tower is certainly one of the country's premier viewpoints; on a clear day it is possible to see 13 counties and enjoy views of the Vale of Evesham, the Vale of Gloucester, the Severn valley and the Welsh mountains. The tower has also had some interesting inhabitants and owners including William Morris and the archaeologist Sir Arthur Evans; at one time it was virtually a country retreat for the pre-Raphaelites.

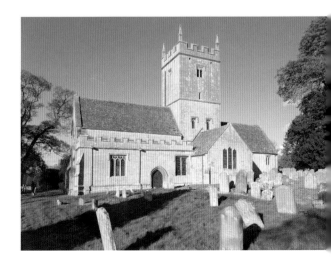

STANTON This is essentially a single street village and is claimed by many to be one of the oldest in the Cotswolds. Most of the houses date from the 17th century but the village was extensively restored by the architect Sir Philip Stott after he purchased large tracts of it just before the First World War. Stott modernised many features but set up covenants to prevent the worst excesses of the 20th century from taking hold. His work means that Stanton often provides a backdrop for period films and television dramatisations. Parts of Stanton's church date back to the 12th century and it features both a 14th-century and a Jacobean pulpit. It has an elegant spire and some of its windows are from the 15th century.

LAVERTON Located beneath the Cotswold edge, Laverton contains several substantial and well-built farmhouses that date back to the 16th century and make good use of local stone. Laverton is close to the Cotswold Way and the many fine views in the area make it popular with walkers. Broadway to the north and Stanton to the south are within easy reach.

STANWAY The village of Stanway is dominated by the gatehouse to Stanway House where a mixture of Gothic, Renaissance and Dutch styles are given a pleasing unity by the local stone. Stanway House was built during the 1580s on the site of an earlier manor house. It is mostly Jacobean in style and the grounds contain a restored water garden which features the highest fountain in England, an impressive tithe barn dating from 1370 and a log-fired brewing house. The church of St Peter retains its Jacobean pulpit but elsewhere has suffered badly at the hands of Victorian restorers. Opposite the driveway to Stanway House is a thatched cricket pavilion. This unusual building was a gift to the village by the author of *Peter Pan*, JM Barrie, who was a frequent visitor to the area.

East Cotswolds

Travelling west from London, this is the gateway to the Cotswolds with beautiful towns, villages and countryside.

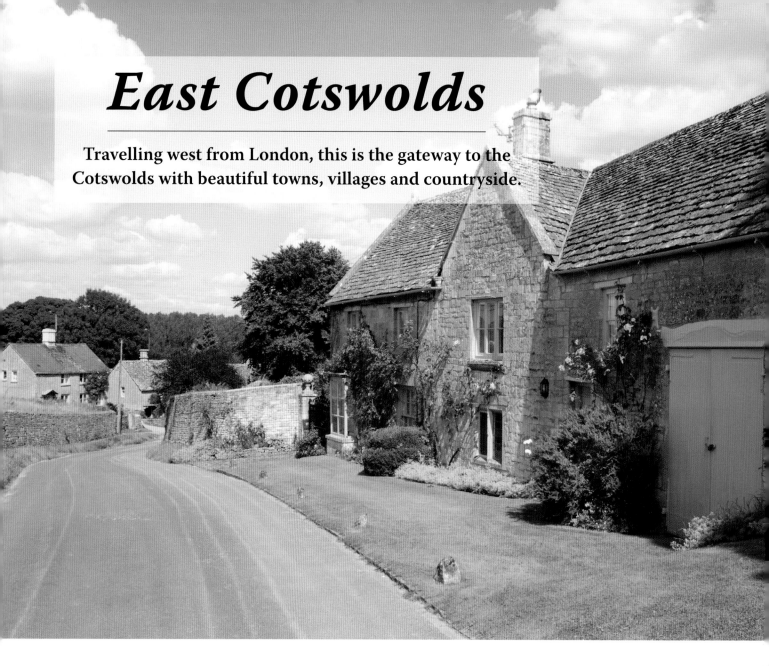

Although much of the Cotswolds is a gently undulating plateau, the area is nevertheless high enough to attract rain from the prevailing westerly winds and the limestone hills act as a natural reservoir. Many streams and rivers emerge in the Cotswolds before making their way down to either the Thames or the Severn valleys. Over the years the rivers have carved out many beautiful valleys; some are steep but many are wide and sheltered. This combination of relatively gentle hills, slow-moving rivers and streams was the basis of the Cotswolds' success as an area for sheep-farming and has combined to create the superb landscape we all know today.

WINDRUSH Named after the river on which it stands, Windrush has a small tree-lined green next to an attractive church. It is a former quarrying village and possesses many fine houses built from local stone. A few of the houses date from the 17th century and one is dated 1668. St Peter's church is of Norman origin and has been Windrush's parish church since 1586. The south doorway is elaborately carved with menacing looking beaked heads which are mixed with the heads of other fantastical beasts. In the churchyard there is a finely decorated wool bale tomb, which represents the source of the deceased's wealth in the form of corded bales of wool. South of the village is the Iron Age hill fort of Windrush Camp.

SHERBORNE During the Middle Ages Sherborne's plentiful water supply made it an ideal centre for sheep-shearing. In fact, at that time there was little else in Sherborne apart from sheep and the Abbot of Winchcombe's summer palace. With the Dissolution of the Monasteries the land passed to the Dutton family and by 1651 Sherborne House had been built. The present Sherborne grew up as an estate village for Sherborne House. The Dutton family remained in residence there until the 1980s when the estate was bequeathed to the National Trust. Sherborne House, which was extensively rebuilt in the 19th century, is now divided into luxury flats and the rest of the estate is dedicated to improved access to the land and nature conservation. Sherborne church is near the park and has a medieval tower and spire; it is chiefly interesting for its many monuments and memorials to the Dutton family.

BLEDINGTON This pretty village (left) is in the Evenlode valley and is built around a wide village green. The church was refurbished in the 15th century out of profits from the wool trade. As well as a very old doorway with its original door, the interior features several 15th-century Perpendicular windows containing stained glass believed to be the work of John Pruddle, the master craftsman who produced the windows of Beauchamp Chapel in Warwick.

BURFORD The eastern gateway to the Cotswolds, Burford built its reputation on wool, quarrying and coaching. Wool was important from the 14th century onwards and the stone from quarries near the town was used in the construction of some of Britain's finest buildings, ranging from Blenheim Palace to St Paul's Cathedral. Burford's heyday as a coaching town came in the 18th century when it was an important stop on routes into Oxford and London; "Burford Bait", the huge meals served by the inns, were famous in the region. Sadly, the coaching trade died away with the advent of the railways, which also bypassed the town. Burford's steep High Street with its many inns is well known but there are many other delightful buildings and features away from the main street. Amongst Burford's most interesting houses are the 17th-century Great House and a row of handsome almshouses which were built in 1457 and partially rebuilt in 1828. The church is interesting both architecturally and historically. The original Norman tower is surmounted by an elegant 15th-century spire and there is also a fine two-storey fan-vaulted south porch. In the interior a memorial carving includes the first representation of Amazonian Indians in England and the font preserves the autograph of a Leveller prisoner who was kept in the church during the Civil War. The Tolsey dates from 1500 and was formerly the place where market tolls were collected; it was also the seat of the borough court. Like many market halls it features a sheltered area and, in modern times, a clock for the convenience of traders. The Tolsey is now a museum which houses many interesting artefacts stretching back to the Roman era.

MINSTER LOVELL This riverside settlement combines an idyllic rural setting with buildings and ruins that reflect the village's interesting past. A bridge across the Windrush leads to the High Street which has a selection of thatched cottages and other Cotswold stone houses. St Kenelm's church was built in 1431 and has an attractive vaulted ceiling underneath the central tower. Some of the stained glass may be original and there is a fine alabaster knight's tomb. Colourful local legends surround the fate of the ninth Lord Lovell who fought with Richard III at Bosworth Field. According to these stories, building work in the early 18th century revealed a vault complete with skeleton. In the mid-18th century the manor was dismantled to provide building stone.

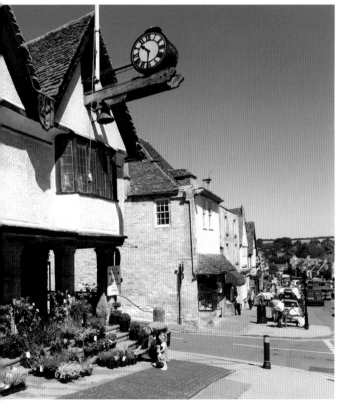

BOURTON-ON-THE-WATER Five ornamental bridges span the river Windrush in Bourton-on-the-Water giving it a unique appeal and the nickname of the "Venice of the Cotswolds". Moving downstream, the five bridges are: Bourton Bridge built in 1806 and widened in 1959; Mill Bridge (also known as Broad Bridge), built in 1654 on the site of a former ford; High Bridge, a footbridge built in 1756; New Bridge (or Moore Bridge) built in 1911 to traverse another ford; and Coronation Bridge, built in 1953 to replace an 18th-century wooden bridge. During the summer, a game of football is attempted between two of the bridges. The goalposts are set in the river and teams play using a standard football. The aim of the game is to score as many goals as possible but the general effect is to get everyone else as wet as possible. Bourton-on-the-Water is served by the parish church of St Lawrence. The only visible part of the old church is the chancel, built in 1328 by Walter de Burhton. In 1784 the Norman church was largely replaced with today's neo-Classical style building with its thick tower housing a clock and bells. Further additions were made in the 1870s when the present nave was constructed. The nave roof is a fine example of a king-post roof.

BOURTON ATTRACTIONS Other places of interest in this popular village include: the Dragonfly Maze with over a quarter of a mile of pathways and an attractive pavilion at its centre; Birdland, a bird sanctuary that includes a small colony of penguins; the Cotswold Motor Museum; and the Model Village which is a ninth scale replica of the village. The model Bourton-on-the-Water contains a model of the model village whilst Bourton-on-the-Water itself also contains a model railway exhibition and Miniature World. On a larger scale visitors can see collections of pottery at the studio in Clapton Row and an exhibition of village life housed in an 18th-century water mill. On the edge of the village is a series of flooded gravel pits which have been established as a nature reserve with a wide variety of bird life.

EASTLEACH MARTIN AND EASTLEACH TURVILLE The two villages at Eastleach, Turville and Martin, face each other across the river Leach. The two villages once belonged to different manors and therefore have their own manor houses and churches. Eastleach Martin has the larger of the churches and its 14th-century north transept is graced with three Decorated-style windows. Eastleach Turville's church has a 14th-century saddleback tower and a Norman tympanum. The two churches are 200 yards apart and the villages are connected by two bridges. One bridge carries the road but the other is an unusual construction of large flat stones. This footbridge is known as Keble's Bridge and commemorates the Keble family who were lords of the manor of Eastleach Turville in the 16th century.

EASTLEACH HISTORY

The most famous member of the Keble family was John who founded the Oxford Movement and after whom Keble College Oxford is named. The peaceful aspect of today's villages makes it difficult to imagine that there were once anti-machinery riots here. By the 19th century wool production had largely been replaced by corn growing and by the 1830s the introduction of threshing machines began to put people out of work. Several machines were destroyed by desperate labourers in the area resulting in imprisonment and transportation for those involved.

FAIRFORD The jewel in Fairford's crown is the church of St Mary. Constructed in the late Perpendicular style it celebrates the wealth and power of the Tame family who built it out of profits from the wool industry. St Mary's stained-glass windows survived 17th-century Puritan purges and are a particularly fine example of late medieval work. Other notable buildings in Fairford include an early 18th century free school decorated with plaques to esteemed teachers, the 17th century Bull Hotel, Fairford Mill and the oxpen.

Around Stroud

This busy market town lies at the heart of five valleys and is surrounded by idyllic countryside and pretty villages.

The Stroud district in the south Cotswolds is famous for its deep wooded valleys, commanding vistas and pretty villages. Stroud itself is built around the intersection of five valleys and is a vibrant town with a long history. The surrounding countryside contains the outstanding villages of Bisley, Woodchester, Miserden, Nailsworth, Minchinhampton and Slad – the village made famous by Laurie Lee in his book *Cider With Rosie*, an evocative portrayal of life in the Slad valley in the 1920s. The 102-mile Cotswolds Way passes through the district between Alderley and Birdlip and gives access to some of the best viewpoints in the Cotswolds such as Coaley Peak and Haresfield Beacon.

CAM LONG DOWN A popular spot for sightseers, Cam Long Down is linked to the main Cotswold escarpment via a saddle to Cam Peak. The top of Cam Long Down forms a narrow plateau which is famous for its wildflowers. The views from the top extend over the river Severn and the curve of the Cotswold escarpment itself. To the south-west can be seen the town of Dursley and to the south the wooded top of Downham Hill, which is known locally as Smallpox Hill. To the south-west stands the Tyndale Monument, dedicated to William Tyndale, first translator of the New Testament into English.

BOWBRIDGE FROM RODBOROUGH The village of Rodborough is on the edge of Stroud and occupies the end of a spur of land which rises to over 600ft (183m). Rodborough church has a stained-glass window depicting Thomas the Tank Engine in memory of the Reverend Wilbert Awdry who lived in the village from 1965 onwards. Rodborough is also home to Winstone's ice cream factory. Above the village is Rodborough Common; the ancient road from London to Stroud used to run across here and provided the village with carriage trade.

COALEY PEAK This picnic site consists of 12 acres of grassland on the edge of the Cotswold escarpment. It was purchased by Gloucestershire County Council in 1972 for public recreation and at that time was mostly arable land; today wildflowers flourish. The site commands wide-ranging views across the Severn Vale and is bordered to the south by the Frocester Hill nature reserve and to the north-east by Stanley Woods. Woodchester Park, a beautiful valley containing a "lost" garden and a chain of five lakes, owned by the National Trust, lies to the east. At the centre of the site is the Nympsfield long barrow, a Neolithic burial chamber dating back to about 2900BC. It was excavated in 1937 and 1974 and the remains of at least 16 skeletons were found.

STROUD Five valleys converge at Stroud making it a natural centre for trade and transport. In the Middle Ages Stroud quickly established itself as a centre of the cloth industry and at the height of its prosperity there were 150 cloth mills in and around the town. Stroud was particularly famous for manufacturing the cloth used in military uniforms. The centre of Stroud reflects its role as a market town with its many narrow streets, its Tudor town hall and the area known as the Shambles which catered for butchers. The neo-Classical Subscription Rooms (built by public subscription in the 19th century) are now a venue for concerts and exhibitions.

STROUD TODAY The decline of the wool trade did not dampen Stroud's spirits overmuch and the area increasingly became a centre for light industry in the late 19th and early 20th centuries. Fortunately, industrial growth has not seriously diminished the town's charm and modern Stroud emphasises its relaxed atmosphere and alternative lifestyles. Stroud now plays host to lively music and dance festivals and to a flourishing arts scene. Pavement cafés and small art galleries are common. The five valleys that meet at Stroud provide easy access to different parts of the Cotswolds and so make the town a good starting point for visitors exploring the area.

SLAD This is a small village that stretches out along the side of a valley north-east of Stroud. It was the childhood home of the author Laurie Lee. Life in the village in the 1920s is brilliantly evoked in Laurie Lee's autobiography *Cider With Rosie* but the present village has not let literary fame go to its head. It remains remarkably unspoiled and it is still possible to gain a sense of the quiet pre-motor car village described by Laurie Lee in the 1920s. Lee's "local", The Wool Pack inn, mentioned in the book, is still trading. The earliest references to Slad come from 1353 when a bridge was built here to cross the Slad Brook, but the oldest building is probably Steanbridge House, an early 17th-century gabled clothier's house. Some weavers' cottages also date from this period but the Church of the Holy Trinity and the village school were built in the 1830s. Laurie Lee is buried in the graveyard of the church.

BISLEY The many fine houses in and around Bisley are a testament to the wealth created by the cloth trade in the 18th century. At one end of the village are five water chutes known locally as "The Wells"; they were restored to commemorate the Reverend Thomas Keble, brother of John, who was rector of Bisley for nearly 50 years. As was common in many Cotswold communities the village has a small 19th-century two-person lock-up; with its ogee-gables Bisley's is a particularly fine example.

MISERDEN Most of the buildings in Miserden are 19th and 20th century in origin but the village has had a long history of growth, decay and renewal. Near to the village are the earthworks of a motte and bailey castle which was erected shortly after the Norman Conquest. The name Miserden is a corruption of the name of the family, la Musarder, that held the manor from the 12th century onwards. Among the surviving 17th-century houses are the rectory, Lampacre cottage and a pair of cottages, one of which used to be the blacksmith's. The two-storey dower house dates from the 18th century and had an east wing added in the 1860s by Sir John Rolt; Sir John also rebuilt other parts of the village. The church has late Saxon origins although it was extensively restored in the 1880s. The war memorial was designed by Sir Edwin Lutyens who also carried out work at Misarden Park, a large Elizabethan mansion with exquisite gardens just to the east of the village. A comparatively recent feature is a small octagonal shelter built in traditional style around a large sycamore tree.

CAUDLE GREEN This delightful hamlet is set in the deeply incised valley of the upper reaches of the river Frome, a mile north-east of Miserden, its larger neighbour. The farm-house facing the village green is a rectangular mid 18th-century building of five bays in ashlar stonework and there are a number of traditional cottages built in Cotswold stone. Walks on the local foot-paths give visitors the impression of being completely cut off from the modern world.

CRANHAM Built at the head of a valley, Cranham enjoys excellent views plus access to a large common to the south and extensive beech woods to the north. The parish church of St James the Great is in the south-western part of the village and dominates the surrounding countryside. It was built largely in the 15th century when the area prospered as a result of sheep-rearing. This is commemorated on the church itself by two pairs of sheep-shears carved onto the second stage of the church tower. Inside the church there is an early 16th-century rood screen and a monument to Obadiah Done who was rector to the parish for 57 years. The composer Gustav Holst lived briefly in Cranham and whilst there wrote what is probably the best-known tune for Christina Rossetti's Christmas carol *In the Bleak Midwinter.* The tune is called Cranham and the house where he stayed is now called Midwinter Cottage. The Cotswold Way footpath runs nearby.

PAINSWICK The stream below Painswick once provided power for its woollen mills whilst its crystal clear water made the village an important centre for cloth dyeing. Many of the houses in the village date from the 17th and 18th centuries and once belonged to wealthy wool merchants. At the centre of the village is a fine church which combines sections from the 15th century with an elegant 17th-century tower. Surrounding the church are well-tended colonnades of yew trees which have been in place since 1792. Local legend has it that there are only 99 trees as the devil always

kills the hundredth. Each year in September the Painswick Clipping Ceremony is held. This has nothing to do with keeping the yews in check but takes its name from the Old English word *clyppan* meaning to embrace. Groups of children form a circle around the church then approach and retreat from it three times whilst singing a hymn. A cake containing a porcelain dog, known as "puppy dog pie" was traditionally baked on this day.

HARESFIELD BEACON Close to Randwick and three miles north-west of Stroud, this popular beauty spot lies on the edge of the Cotswold escarpment. The Cotswold Way national trail runs along the escarpment. The 429 acre Haresfield estate, made up of beech woodland and open grassland, and which includes Haresfield Beacon, is owned by the National Trust. Haresfield Beacon is the site of a Romano-British hill fort and has wonderful views across the Severn Vale, including the village from which it takes its name. The nearby hamlet of Harescombe consists of a scattering of farms and cottages with the beautifully situated church of St John the Baptist at the foot of the rising hills.

MINCHINHAMPTON This attractive village, centred on its High Street and old Market Square, was once one of the most important cloth towns in the Cotswolds. Minchinhampton was not easily accessible by road and this meant that it retained more of its old-fashioned charm than many similar towns. The square is dominated by the 17th-century Market House which is supported on sturdy stone pillars. Nearby is a post office which is housed in a Queen Anne building. Parts of the church date from the 12th century but the top of the spire had to be removed to prevent collapse in 1863. The truncated stub has been finished with an unusual "coronet". Of particular interest in the interior is the 14th-century south transept which contains a varied collection of tomb recesses and effigies in the Decorated style.

MINCHINHAMPTON COMMON

The 600-acre Minchinhampton Common was granted to the people of the village in the 16th century to encourage the settlement of skilled people. A weaver was allowed to enclose land on it and build a cottage. The common is now owned and managed by the National Trust and its elevated location makes it a popular destination for ramblers. As well as being a popular recreation area the common contains several important archaeological sites. The most visible and extensive Iron Age remains slightly pre-date the Roman conquest and indicate that the area was a strategic location for the Dobunni tribe. Known as the Bulwarks these large defensive earthworks are over a mile long. Nearby is Amberley Camp which is a hill fort enclosing around 50 acres. There are also many round and long barrows and other prehistoric remains in the area.

AMBERLEY The village commands splendid views over the steep valley of the Nailsworth stream and is located on the western edge of Minchinhampton Common. The village today is a scattered settlement that has taken various guises since the Middle Ages. Most of the older buildings in the area are former weaver's cottages.

WOODCHESTER Divided into North and South
Woodchester, this elegant village lies in the valley of the
Nailsworth stream two miles south of Stroud. To the south-
west is Woodchester Park which contains the ruins of a
large 19th-century mansion. The building was instigated by
William Leigh, a wealthy merchant, who purchased the park
in 1846. Leigh wanted to live in a Gothic Revival mansion
and approached several architects including Pugin to plan
his new home. Construction began in 1858 and continued
until 1870 but when William Leigh died in 1873 all work
stopped. Some parts of the never-completed house were
occupied by Leigh's family and at various times it served
as a mental health hospital and a teacher-training college.
Shortly after the Second World War the house was aban-
doned but fortunately it never completely fell into ruins. The
Woodchester Mansion Trust took over the building in 1992
and it is now open to the public. The Trust also provides
training on stone conservation and other traditional crafts.

WOODCHESTER'S ORIGINS The village of Woodchester grew up as a processing centre for the wool industry and between 1750 and 1820 there were 10 mills in the Woodchester area. The plentiful supplies of water in the valley provided power for the mills as well as for fulling and dyeing. A napping machine was invented at Southfields Mill and opposite Frogmarsh Mill is the unique 16th-century Teasel Tower. Its name derives from the fact that it was used to store the teasels (dried prickly plant heads) used to raise the nap on cloth. Also in Woodchester are the remains of a large Roman villa. Excavations in St Mary's churchyard in the 18th century revealed a beautiful mosaic pavement showing the Orpheus story. A replica was made by brothers John and Bob Woodward which for a time was on display at Prinknash Abbey. In June 2010 the replica was sold at auction for £75,000.

AVENING The medieval village of Avening grew up around the Norman church of the Holy Rood. Dating from 1080 and occupying the site of an earlier Saxon church, Holy Rood has several points of interest for those who venture inside. The south transept houses a small museum that has models of the church at various periods of its life as well as a Saxon skeleton and some wild boar tusks. One of the monuments is dedicated to a former pirate. Avening also boasts a number of substantial buildings built out of the profits of the wool trade. Local streams once provided power for a mill and water for cloth processing. Just above the village are three burial chambers excavated from a nearby long barrow in 1806.

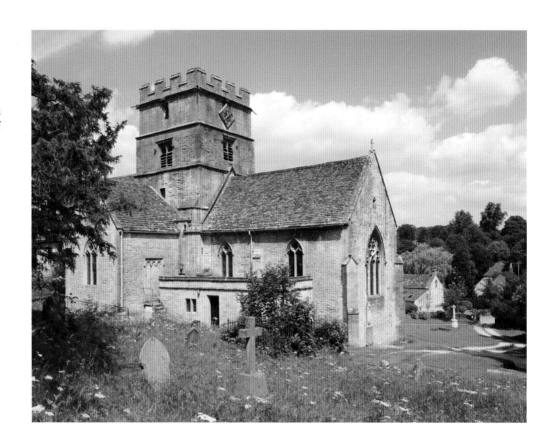

OWLPEN The Owlpen Manor estate includes the manor itself, a 19th-century church and a number of cottages nearby. With an adult population of around 35 the parish of Owlpen is the smallest in Gloucestershire. The manor house dates from 1450 to 1616 and features a Tudor Great Hall and a Great Chamber. Owlpen Manor is reputedly haunted by Margaret of Anjou, the queen consort of Henry VI. She is said to appear as a lady in beautiful clothes drifting through the rooms of the house. Margaret stayed at Owlpen Manor in 1471 before the Battle of Tewkesbury, which her faction lost. The restoration of Owlpen was undertaken by Norman Jewson who bought the house in the 1920s but unfortunately could not afford to live in it thereafter.

NAILSWORTH This village is about three miles south of Stroud in one of that town's five valleys. Nailsworth is itself at the meeting place of three valleys which branch off towards Avening, Horsley and Stroud. The village's plentiful water supply enabled the construction of large woollen mills and one of them, Egypt Mill, has now been restored with its water wheels and most of its gearing still intact. The building now operates as a restaurant.

NYMPSFIELD A small village at the head of a valley near the Cotswold edge, Nympsfield developed along the route of a former Roman road from Cirencester to Arlingham. The village grew up as a busy stopping place on a coaching route and in its heyday there were five inns in the village catering for passing trade. Nympsfield long barrow has been extensively excavated and is open to the sky allowing visitors to see the interior of this ancient burial place.

South Cotswolds

Dotted with charming villages, the southern Cotswolds includes Castle Combe, much loved for its beautiful setting and architecture.

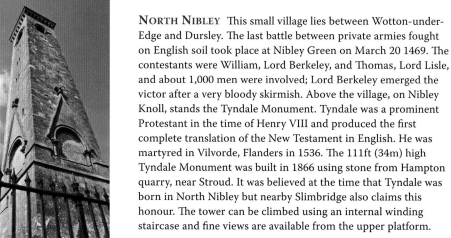

The south Cotswolds has more than its fair share of beautiful countryside and pretty villages. Some of the prettiest villages such as Castle Combe are strictly outside of what many people would regard as the boundaries of the Cotswolds. However, they are to all intents and purposes Cotswold settlements with honey-coloured buildings, a strong sense of wool-farming history and proximity to the Cotswold edge.

NORTH NIBLEY This small village lies between Wotton-under-Edge and Dursley. The last battle between private armies fought on English soil took place at Nibley Green on March 20 1469. The contestants were William, Lord Berkeley, and Thomas, Lord Lisle, and about 1,000 men were involved; Lord Berkeley emerged the victor after a very bloody skirmish. Above the village, on Nibley Knoll, stands the Tyndale Monument. Tyndale was a prominent Protestant in the time of Henry VIII and produced the first complete translation of the New Testament in English. He was martyred in Vilvorde, Flanders in 1536. The 111ft (34m) high Tyndale Monument was built in 1866 using stone from Hampton quarry, near Stroud. It was believed at the time that Tyndale was born in North Nibley but nearby Slimbridge also claims this honour. The tower can be climbed using an internal winding staircase and fine views are available from the upper platform.

TETBURY Dominating Tetbury is its 17th-century Market House. This imposing building is supported on three rows of pillars and has a stone roof; it used to be higher but it was reduced by one storey in 1817. Above the roof is a fine cupola on which there is a weather vane decorated with gilded

dolphins. The dolphins also appear on the town's coat of arms. Near to the Market House are the Chipping Steps, where a livestock market took place amongst an imposing collection of 18th and 19th-century buildings. Also in this area is Gumstool Hill where the annual Woolsack Races take place every spring bank holiday Monday. This rather gruelling event involves contestants running down Gumstool Hill (one-in-four) and up again carrying a 60lb (27kg) woolsack. Teams of young men and women – the women's sacks are only 35lb (16kg) – take part in the race whilst towns-people dress up in medieval costumes. In 1633 the town was sold to four local

residents who became known as the Feoffees. Along with 13 town wardens the Feoffees virtually ran Tetbury; today they confine themselves to charitable activities. St Mary's church is an imposing building rebuilt in the Gothic style in the late 18th century; its spire is 186ft (57m) high. The interior is illuminated by graceful Perpendicular windows and it features box pews, panelled galleries and two magnificent chandeliers. Tetbury's original courthouse now houses a Police Museum which tells the story of the Gloucestershire Police Constabulary since its founding in 1839. Visitors can inspect cells, the original police office and the magistrate's court.

OZLEWORTH Set in a quiet wooded valley overlooking Newark Park, the small group of buildings that comprise Ozleworth can be approached through Ozleworth Park. The Norman church stands in a churchyard which in itself is a sign of an earlier religious site, possibly a sacred grove. The church of St Nicholas has an extremely rare hexagonal central tower dating from the early 12th century combined with a nave that was added in the 1220s. The stairway to the musicians' gallery fits into the thickness of the wall, an arrangement that consider-ably weakens its structure.

WOTTON-UNDER-EDGE The principal buildings of this fine town are laid out on a grid plan rather than being clustered around a central square or green. This arrangement may have been an early experiment in town planning as it was carried out at the behest of Joan de Somery, the lady of the manor who granted the town its charter in 1253. The town's oldest building is the timber-framed Ram Inn which is believed to date from 1350. The parish church of St Mary the Virgin was consecrated in 1283 and possesses a fine late 14th-century tower. Inside the church is the Berkeley tomb, an early 15th-century table tomb with life-sized brasses (reputedly the best of their kind in England) of Thomas, 10th Baron de Berkeley (1352-1417), and his wife, Margaret. One of the first grammar schools in the country was founded at Wotton by Katharine Lady Berkeley in 1384. One notable resident of Wotton was Sir Isaac Pitman who lived in a house that still stands in Orchard Street.

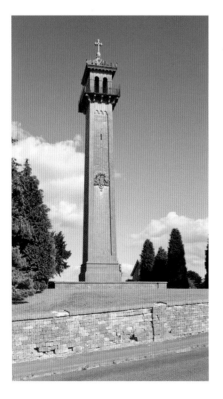

HAWKESBURY The village of Hawkesbury nestles in a wooded coombe below the Cotswold scarp. It is dominated by its parish church which dates back to the 12th century and is on the site of an earlier Saxon church. It is mainly in the Perpendicular style. The promise of the exterior is not matched by the interior which was rather over-improved from 1882-85. The Old Vicarage to the east of the church is an unusual L-shape and dates from the late 15th century. It features a two-storey gabled porch and a late 18th-century garden building with Gothic arched windows. Outside the village on the Cotswold edge is the Somerset Monument. This was erected in 1846 to commemorate General Lord Edward Somerset who served with distinction at Waterloo and died in 1842. Somerset was the nephew of the sixth Duke of Beaufort whose family home is at nearby Badminton.

GREAT AND LITTLE BADMINTON Situated some 400ft (122m) up on the Cotswolds, both Badminton villages enjoy extensive views across the surrounding area. Great Badminton is famous for the annual horse trials that take place at Badminton House. Great Badminton is an estate village which means that it grew up serving the needs of nearby Badminton House. The bulk of the houses in the present village date from the late 18th and early 19th centuries. Little Badminton is just to the north of Great Badminton and although its buildings are slightly scattered it has the village green as a focal point. Badminton House is the home of the Beaufort family and is a particularly fine example of the Palladian period.

CASTLE COMBE Although well to the south of the traditional Cotswold area, Castle Combe displays many of the charms of the area and is a popular destination for visitors. The village is centred on a market cross that reflects its growth through wool-trading. Other marks of this once-great industry include several fine timber-framed buildings clustered around the cross and the substantial Perpendicular tower that was added to the church in 1434. The village is situated on the By Brook and there is a charming bridge that spans the stream here. The Norman castle that gives the village its name has largely disappeared but signs of it, such as the mound on which it was built, are still present.

VILLAGE ATTRACTIONS The photogenic charm of Castle Combe has regularly attracted film-makers. In 1966 a section of the By Brook near the bridge was converted into a miniature port complete with jetty and boats for the filming of *Dr Doolittle*.

More recently Robert de Niro and Sienna Miller visited the village for the making of *Stardust*. There are many fine walks including the Macmillan Way long-distance footpath. Also nearby is the Castle Combe motor racing circuit which opened in 1950 on the site of a former air base.

COLD ASHTON MANOR

Cold Ashton is situated on the southern edge of the Cotswolds and, given the literalism of much of the naming in the area, it probably derives its name from the cold winds that sweep in over the Bristol Channel. However, most people would probably be happy to tolerate the chilly location for the splendid views that its elevation affords. Cold Ashton Manor is a large gabled building dating from the Jacobean period. It was probably erected by John Gunning, a former mayor of Bristol, in 1629. The Renaissance archway leading onto the road has square Roman Doric columns with a rosette frieze. These are surmounted by two flower-filled urns with semi-circular steps leading down from it.

MARSHFIELD Another literally named town, although this may not be obvious to modern ears; it simply means a field on the march, or edge. The tower of the parish church dominates the skyline for several miles around and provides a reference point for walkers. An original Norman building, it was rebuilt in the Perpendicular style in about 1470. Further restorations took place in the late 19th and early 20th centuries.

The town contains a splendid mixture of building styles ranging from a Georgian-Gothic tollhouse through to a medieval barn and dovecote to an early Georgian stable range. Marshfield benefits from its proximity to Bath and Bristol and has been a market town since 1234. In the Middle Ages it was one of the largest towns in the area and its prosperity continued well into the 18th century. By then it was particularly concerned with the malt trade as can be seen in the many malt houses and long storage buildings at the back of some properties. Of the listed buildings in the town the almshouses established by the Crispe family between 1612 and 1619 are particularly interesting. The eight gabled houses are arranged on either side of a chapel. Originally each house consisted of a single room with a stone spiral staircase in one corner leading to a bedroom.

Bath

Largely constructed from beautiful Cotswold stone, the World Heritage city of Bath is a feast of Georgian and Regency architecture.

The elegant city of Bath has had two major heydays. The first was during the Roman occupation when the town of *Aqua Sulis* grew up around the natural hot springs in the area and the second was during the Regency and Georgian periods when the craze for taking the waters made Bath the centre of fashion and one of the largest cities in England. Substantial traces of both periods can still be seen in the city today. Bath is on the very edge of the Cotswold hills and the stone in this area is usually described as creamy rather than golden. The Roman temple and baths, the abbey and the city's famous crescents are all built from locally quarried limestone. Apart from the Roman baths and the temple, the ancient city of Bath largely disappeared during

the Saxon period and the city was largely in royal and monastic hands throughout the Middle Ages. The spa trade began to revive after the Dissolution of the Monasteries but it was not until after the Civil War that Bath began to be a health centre for the aristocracy. The new Bath was largely built in the Classical style with long stretches of identical façades to give impressions of palatial scale and classical decorum.

The pretty shop housing Sally Lunn's tea room is the oldest house in Bath and dates from around 1482.

BATH SPA The Romans named Bath *Aquae Sulis* and made use of the natural hot springs to indulge their passion for bathing. But it was during the 18th century that the popularity of "taking the waters" exploded and the rich and powerful made their way to the city to frolic in the waters. In 1706 a Pump Room was built so that visitors could drink the water. This neo-Classical salon became a centre for the social life of the town for more than two centuries. Bath quickly developed a reputation for freedom and licentiousness. The town became a place where unattached men or women could attract a future spouse. And free from the social confines of their home lives, many visitors quickly forgot any health reasons for their visit and indulged in gossip and "unlikely" social liaisons. Now the baths have been fully modernised with the addition of a large glass extension which houses up-to-date spa treatments and interlinks with the historic spa buildings.

First published in 2011 by Myriad Books Limited
35 Bishopsthorpe Road, London SE26 4PA

Photographs copyright © Stephen Dorey
Text copyright © John Mannion

ISBN 1 84746 391 6
EAN 978 1 84746 391 3

Designed by Jerry Goldie Graphic Design

Printed in China

www.myriadbooks.com